PIANO • VOCAL • GUITAR

CHART HITS OF '96-'97

ISBN 0-7935-7703-9

HAL•LEONARD®
CORPORATION

7777 W. BLUEMOUND RD. P.O. BOX 13819 MILWAUKEE, WI 53213

Visit Hal Leonard Online at
www.halleonard.com

CONTENTS

ALWAYS BE MY BABY

Words and Music by MARIAH CAREY,
JERMAINE DUPRI and MANUEL SEAL

We were as one, _ babe for a mo-ment in ____ time. _
I ain't gon-na cry, _ no, and I won't beg you to ____ stay. _

And it seemed ev - er - last - ing, that you would al - ways be mine.
If you're de - ter-mined to leave_ boy, I will not stand in your way.

Now you want to be free,_____ so I'll let you fly,_____
But in - ev - i - ta - bly _____ you'll be back a - gain,_____

'cause I know in my heart,_ babe, our love will nev - er die. _
'cause you know in your heart,_ babe, our love will nev - er end. _

You'll al - ways be a part of me. _ I'm part of you in - def - i - nite - ly.

BIRMINGHAM

Words and Music by DAVID TYSON,
DEAN McTAGGART and GERALD O'BRIEN

Virgil Spence has got a nine-teen inch Hi-ta-chi
It's three A. M. and Vir-gil's passed out on the so-fa,

and man-y de-mons lin-ger-ing.
a fifth of Jim Beam on the floor.

Fri-day night he pulled a gun to change the chan-nel,
She's packed a bag. She slips the keys out of his pock-et.

To Coda

bam - a moon. _____ She's look - ing for ___ the prom - ised land _____

out be - yond the lights of Bir - ming - ham. _____ An -

Bir - ming - ham. _____

Lead vocal ad lib.

Repeat and Fade

BLUE

Words and Music by
BILL MACK

CHANGE THE WORLD

featured on the Motion Picture Soundtrack PHENOMENON

Words and Music by GORDON KENNEDY,
TOMMY SIMS and WAYNE KIRKPATRICK

FREE TO DECIDE

Lyrics and Music by
DOLORES O'RIORDAN

COUNTING BLUE CARS

Words by J.R. RICHARDS
Music by SCOT ALEXANDER, GEORGE PENDERGAST,
RODNEY BROWNING, J.R. RICHARDS
and GREGORY KOLANEK

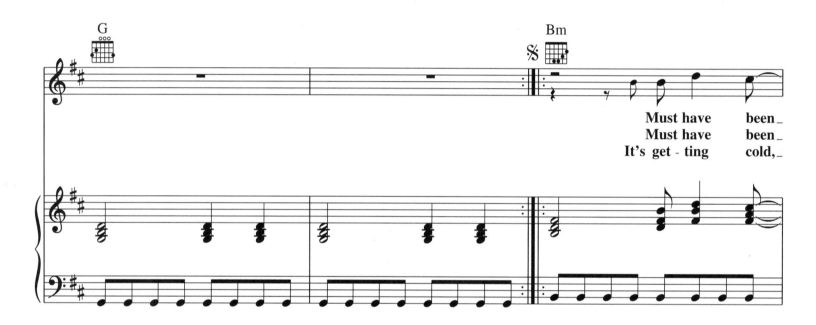

Must have   been _
Must have   been _
It's get - ting   cold, _

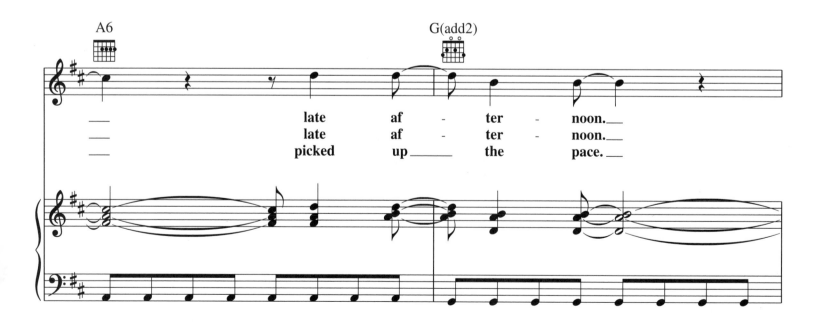

late   af - ter - noon. _
late   af - ter - noon. _
picked   up ____ the   pace. _

GIVE ME ONE REASON

Words and Music by
TRACY CHAPMAN

Tune guitar down one half step.

I FINALLY FOUND SOMEONE

from THE MIRROR HAS TWO FACES

Words and Music by BARBRA STREISAND, MARVIN HAMLISCH,
R. J. LANGE and BRYAN ADAMS

I BELIEVE IN YOU AND ME
from the Touchstone Motion Picture THE PREACHER'S WIFE

Words and Music by DAVID WOLFERT
and SANDY LINZER

IF WE FALL IN LOVE TONIGHT

Words and Music by JAMES HARRIS III
and TERRY LEWIS

be all right. _ Your heart is in good hands. _ Dar - lin',

if, _____ if ___ we fall in love a - gain, _ on ___ me you

can de - pend, _ if you can take a chance. _

O - pen _ your heart and _ let love love a - gain. _

Repeat and Fade

IT'S ALL COMING BACK TO ME NOW

Words and Music by
JIM STEINMAN

INSENSITIVE

Words and Music by
ANNE LOREE

How do you cool ____ your lips
How do you numb ____ your skin

IRONIC

Lyrics by ALANIS MORISSETTE
Music by ALANIS MORISSETTE
and GLEN BALLARD

KEY WEST INTERMEZZO

(I SAW YOU FIRST)

Words and Music by GEORGE M. GREEN
and JOHN MELLENCAMP

This loud Cu - ban ___ band ___ is cru - ci - fy - ing John

Len - non.   No one wants_to be lone - ly.

No one wants_to sing the blues.

She's perched like a par - rot   on his tux - e - do shoul -
On a   mud - spat - tered road,   in her fa - v'rite re - bo -
In the   bold - col - ored dawn,   me and Gyp - sy's god is

LAST NIGHT

Words and Music by BABYFACE
and KEITH ANDES

LET'S MAKE A NIGHT TO REMEMBER

Words and Music by BRYAN ADAMS
and ROBERT JOHN LANGE

1. I love the way ya look to - night, _
(Verse 2 see block lyric)

with your hair hang-in' down on your shoul - ders. _____

(ad lib. vocal)

Play 5 times for fade

Verse 2:

I love the way ya move tonight.
Beads of sweat drippin' down your skin.
Me lying here n' you lyin' there.
Our shadows on the wall and our hands everywhere.

Let's make out, let's do something amazing.
Let's do something that's all the way.
'Cuz I've never touched somebody
Like the way I touch your body.
Now I never want to let your body go.

Let's make a night to remember, *etc.*

MISSION: IMPOSSIBLE THEME
from the Paramount Motion Picture MISSION: IMPOSSIBLE

Music by LALO SCHIFRIN

Moderate Dance beat, with drive

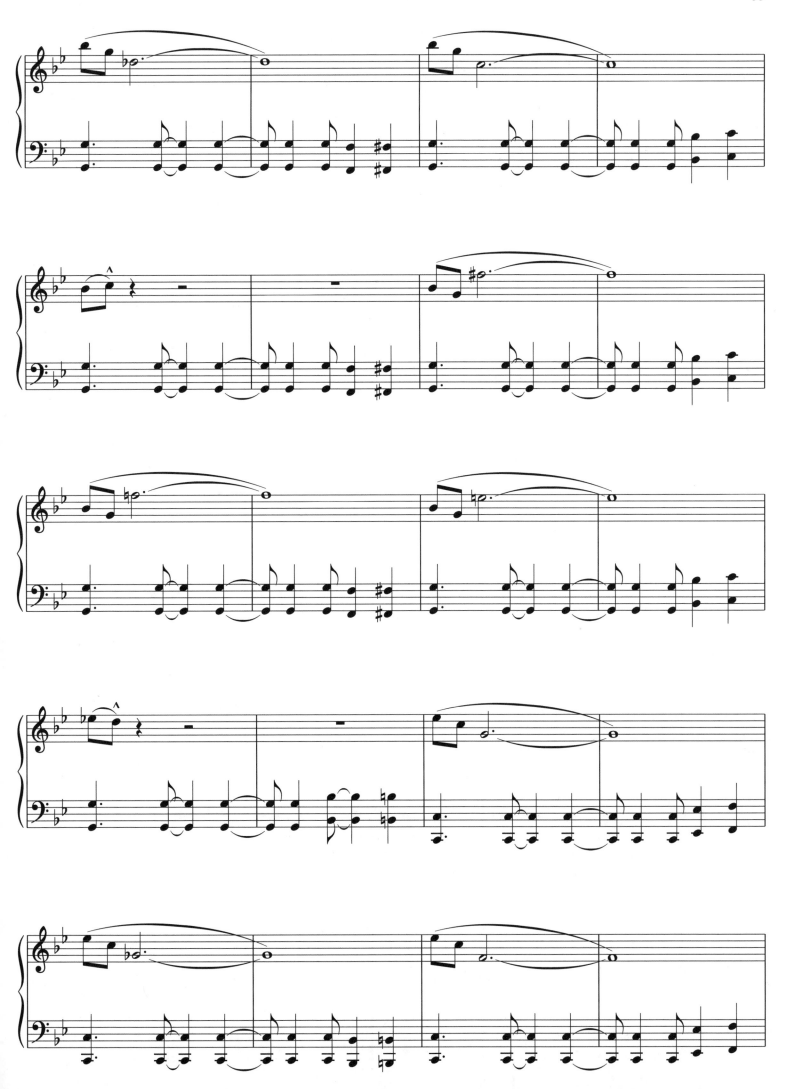

To Coda ⊕

THE MOMENT

By KENNY G

Slowly, tenderly

MOUTH

Words and Music by
MERRIL BAINBRIDGE

MCA music publishing

NAME

Words and Music by
JOHN RZEZNIK

Instrumental solo - ad lib.

ONE SWEET DAY

Words and Music by MARIAH CAREY, WALTER AFANASIEFF, SHAWN STOCKMAN, MICHAEL McCARY, NATHAN MORRIS and WANYA MORRIS

REAL LOVE

Words and Music by
JOHN LENNON

SOMEDAY
from Walt Disney's THE HUNCHBACK OF NOTRE DAME

Music by ALAN MENKEN
Lyrics by STEPHEN SCHWARTZ

THAT THING YOU DO!

from the Original Motion Picture Soundtrack THAT THING YOU DO!

Words and Music by
ADAM SCHLESINGER

WHAT KIND OF MAN WOULD I BE

Words and Music by
LAWRENCE WADDELL

WHERE DO YOU GO

Words and Music by G. MART,
PETER BISCHOF-FALLENSTEIN and JAMES WALLS

Moderately fast Dance tempo

You got-ta break the si - lence; don't _ keep me wait -

- ing.

De - spite the riv - er flow -

- ing to ___ the sea, you're run-ning back to me. ___ Come hear what I'm say -

- ing.

Where do you go, ____ my love -

Instrumental solo - (Vocal tacet)

YOU CAN MAKE HISTORY
(YOUNG AGAIN)

Words and Music by ELTON JOHN
and BERNIE TAUPIN

YOU LEARN

Lyrics by ALANIS MORISSETTE
Music by ALANIS MORISSETTE
and GLEN BALLARD

MCA music publishing

CODA

You grieve, you learn, you choke, you learn,

you laugh, you learn, you choose,___ you learn,___ you pray, you learn,

you ask, you learn, you live, you learn.___

YOU MUST LOVE ME
from the film EVITA

Lyric by TIM RICE
Music by ANDREW LLOYD WEBBER

Additional Lyrics

Verse 2: *(Instrumental 8 bars)*
Why are you at my side?
How can I be any use to you now?
Give me a chance and I'll let you see how
Nothing has changed.
Deep in my heart I'm concealing
Things that I'm longing to say,
Scared to confess what I'm feeling
Frightened you'll slip away,
You must love me.

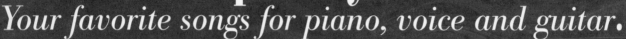

Contemporary Classics
Your favorite songs for piano, voice and guitar.

The Definitive Rock 'n' Roll Collection

A classic collection of the best songs from the early rock 'n' roll years – 1955-1966. 97 songs, including: Barbara Ann • Chantilly Lace • Dream Lover • Duke Of Earl • Earth Angel • Great Balls Of Fire • Louie, Louie • Rock Around The Clock • Ruby Baby • Runaway • (Seven Little Girls) Sitting In The Back Seat • Stay • Surfin' U.S.A. • Wild Thing • Woolly Bully • and more.

00490195 ....$24.95

The Big Book Of Rock

78 of rock's biggest hits, including: Addicted To Love • American Pie • Born To Be Wild • Cold As Ice • Dust In The Wind • Free Bird • Goodbye Yellow Brick Road • Groovin' • Hey Jude • I Love Rock N Roll • Lay Down Sally • Layla • Livin' On A Prayer • Louie Louie • Maggie May • Me And Bobby McGee • Monday, Monday • Owner Of A Lonely Heart • Shout • Walk This Way • We Didn't Start The Fire • You Really Got Me • and more.

00311566..$19.95

Big Book Of Movie And TV Themes

Over 90 familiar themes, including: Alfred Hitchcock Theme • Beauty And The Beast • Candle On The Water • Theme From *E.T.* • Endless Love • Hawaii Five-O • I Love Lucy • Theme From *Jaws* • Jetsons • Major Dad Theme • The Masterpiece • Mickey Mouse March • The Munsters Theme • Theme From *Murder, She Wrote* • Mystery • Somewhere Out There • Unchained Melody • Won't You Be My Neighbor • and more!

00311582 ....$19.95

The Best Rock Songs Ever

70 of the best rock songs from yesterday and today, including: All Day And All Of The Night • All Shook Up • Ballroom Blitz • Bennie And The Jets • Blue Suede Shoes • Born To Be Wild • Boys Are Back In Town • Every Breath You Take • Faith • Free Bird • Hey Jude • I Still Haven't Found What I'm Looking For • Livin' On A Prayer • Lola • Louie Louie • Maggie May • Money • (She's) Some Kind Of Wonderful • Takin' Care Of Business • Walk This Way • We Didn't Start The Fire • We Got The Beat • Wild Thing • more!

00490424 ....$16.95

The Best Of 90s Rock

30 songs, including: Alive • I'd Do Anything For Love (But I Won't Do That) • Livin' On The Edge • Losing My Religion • Two Princes • Walking On Broken Glass • Wind Of Change • and more.

00311668 ....$14.95

35 Classic Hits

35 contemporary favorites, including: Beauty And The Beast • Dust In The Wind • Just The Way You Are • Moon River • The River Of Dreams • Somewhere Out There • Tears In Heaven • When I Fall In Love • A Whole New World (Aladdin's Theme) • and more.

00311654 ....$12.95

55 Contemporary Standards

55 favorites, including: Alfie • Beauty And The Beast • Can't Help Falling In Love • Candle In The Wind • Have I Told You Lately • How Am I Supposed To Live Without You • Memory • The River Of Dreams • Sea Of Love • Tears In Heaven • Up Where We Belong • When I Fall In Love • and more.

00311670 ....$15.95

Women of Modern Rock

25 songs from contemporary chanteuses, including: As I Lay Me Down • Connection • Feed The Tree • Galileo • Here And Now • Look What Love Has Done • Love Sneakin' Up On You • Walking On Broken Glass • You Oughta Know • Zombie • and more.

00310093 ....$14.95

Jock Rock Hits

32 stadium-shaking favorites, including: Another One Bites The Dust • The Boys Are Back In Town • Freeze-Frame • Gonna Make You Sweat (Everybody Dance Now) • I Got You (I Feel Good) • Na Na Hey Hey Kiss Him Goodbye • Rock & Roll – Part II (The Hey Song) • Shout • Tequila • We Are The Champions • We Will Rock You • Whoomp! (There It Is) • Wild Thing • and more.

00310105 ....$14.95

Rock Ballads

31 sentimental favorites, including: All For Love • Bed Of Roses • Dust In The Wind • Everybody Hurts • Right Here Waiting • Tears In Heaven • and more.

00311673 ....$14.95

For More Information, See Your Local Music Dealer,
Or Write To:

HAL•LEONARD®
C O R P O R A T I O N

777 W. Bluemound Rd. P.O. Box 13819 Milwaukee, WI 53213

Visit Hal Leonard Online at www.halleonard.com

Prices, contents & availability subject to change without notice.